WILD·WORLD·OF·AN

SEASHORES

MICHAEL CHINERY
ILLUSTRATED BY WAYNE FORD, MICK LOATES
AND MYKE TAYLOR

Kingfisher Books

Kingfisher Books, Grisewood & Dempsey Ltd,
Elsley House, 24–30 Great Titchfield Street,
London W1P 7AD

First published in 1992 by Kingfisher Books

BRITISH LIBRARY CATALOGUING-IN-PUBLICATION DATA
A catalogue record for this book is available from
the British Library

ISBN 0 86272 916 5

Series editor: Mike Halson
Series designer: Terry Woodley
Designer: Dave West Children's Books
Illustrators: Norman Michael Fahy (p. 38); Wayne Ford
(pp. 1–3, 12–13, 17, 27, 29, 32–3); Mick Loates/*Linden
Artists* (pp. 8, 14, 20–21, 28, 34); Myke Taylor/*Garden
Studio* (pp. 4–7, 9–11, 15–16, 18–19, 22–26, 30–31,
35–37)
Cover illustrations: John Butler

Phototypeset by Southern Positives and Negatives
(SPAN), Lingfield, Surrey.
Printed and bound by Cambus Litho Ltd, East Kilbride.

Contents

Life on the seashores

Seashores are not all the same. They vary depending on the kind of rock forming the coast. Hard rocks form rugged headlands and rocky beaches, but softer rocks are more likely to produce sandy bays. The animals of these two kinds of seashores are very different. Rocky shores are great for exploring at low tide because hundreds of different animals cling to the rocks and seaweeds. Animals that live on sandy shores have to burrow into the sand when the tide goes out, and this makes the beach look rather empty.

 DO YOU KNOW

The tides that sweep in and out over the beaches twice a day are produced by the Sun and the Moon. The highest tides are when the Sun and Moon are both pulling in the same direction.

Waves are made by the wind blowing over the sea and rippling the surface. The stronger the winds, the higher the waves.

On a rocky shore, seaweeds provide vital food and shelter for many animals. When the tide goes out, most of the animals hide away or fix their shells tightly to the rocks – but where there are rock pools you can watch some seashore creatures moving about in the water.

THE STRAND LINE

Every time the tide sweeps over the beach it brings with it a fascinating collection of seaweed and other bits and pieces. This junk stays behind and forms the strand line, marking the high-tide level once the tide has gone out. It is a good place to look for small seashore animals.

MANGROVE SWAMPS

Many tropical sea-shores are fringed with small trees called mangroves. These trees all have masses of branching roots, looking like upturned baskets. The roots anchor them in the shifting mud and sand. Mangrove swamps are home to huge numbers of crabs and birds.

Screaming seagulls

Most seagulls are plump white birds with grey wings. They can be found on nearly all the world's seashores, and often follow ships. Seagulls are great scavengers and eat just about anything. They are always screaming at each other and squabbling over food. Some never go to sea at all and spend all their time at rubbish dumps and on farms. Huge flocks of gulls follow ploughs across the fields and snap up the worms and insects that are uncovered. Three of the commonest seagulls are shown here.

SEAGULL FACTS

● There are about 45 kinds of seagulls. The great black-backed is the biggest. It is 80 cm long and its wings are over 150 cm across.

● The smallest gull is the little gull, which is only 28 cm long.

● Seagulls can live for well over 30 years.

The black-headed gull has no dark head feathers in winter – just a dark smudge behind each eye.

Black-headed gulls find plenty of food among the debris in the strand line. They live mainly in Eurasia.

Seagulls use their webbed feet to paddle around on the surface like ducks, but they rarely dive.

The great black-backed gull of the North Atlantic is as big as a goose. It eats fish, but also takes eggs and chicks from other gulls' nests. It even kills adult birds and rabbits.

Most young gulls are heavily speckled with brown. They may not get their proper adult colours until they are about four years old.

The long, narrow wings are ideal for soaring and gliding in strong wind. Gulls can glide for long periods of time.

The herring gull is a very common gull, found on seashores all round the Northern Hemisphere. Its fluffy chicks look much like those of other gulls. The chicks start to fly when they are about six weeks old.

Hungry chicks peck at the red spot on the adult herring gull's beak, and this makes the adult cough up some food for them.

The strong-armed starfish

The starfish has no head and no real brain. It has a mouth on the underside of its body, and usually has five arms. The underside of each arm is covered with little water-filled suckers called tube-feet. These are very strong and they help the starfish to move and to capture food. Shellfish are the starfish's favourite prey.

DO YOU KNOW

The starfish has a wonderful ability to repair any injury. If it loses an arm, it simply grows a new one, as you can see here. A torn-off arm can even grow a new body!

The starfish moves over the seabed by fixing its suckers to the rocks and then pulling itself forward.

The starfish's strong suckers can easily pull the two halves of a mussel's shell apart. The starfish's mouth then gets to work on the mussel's soft body.

The marine iguana

The marine iguana is the only lizard that regularly takes a dip in the sea. It lives on rocky shores and goes into the sea to browse on seaweeds at low tide. It has partly webbed feet and is a good swimmer, but it does not go far out to sea. It clings to the rocks with its strong claws while feeding, so that the waves do not wash it away. Marine iguanas live only on the Galapagos Islands in the Pacific Ocean.

DO YOU KNOW

Red crabs often scuttle over basking iguanas and sometimes appear to pinch them. The iguanas do not mind, because the crabs are actually pulling blood-sucking ticks from their skin to eat them.

The iguana's sharp teeth are used for tearing the tough seaweeds away from the rocks.

IGUANA FACTS

● The marine iguana is about 1 metre long. Most individuals are plain black or grey.

● When alarmed, the iguana puffs water vapour from its nose – like a fairy-tale dragon.

Stinging sea anemones

Sea anemones grow on rocks and look more like flowers than animals. Their tentacles, or arms, carry poisonous stings, some of which can be very painful to people. The stings are used to catch fish and other small animals. When the prey has been stung, the arms hold it firmly and push it into the anemone's mouth. You can watch the action by tying a piece of meat to some string and dangling it among the tentacles: it is difficult to pull the meat out again.

ANEMONE FACTS

● The biggest sea anemones are about 60 cm across. They live on the coral reefs of Australia.

● Sea anemones often split in half to produce two new animals.

● Some anemones can live for 100 years.

Plumose anemones have so many fine tentacles that they look like feather dusters. They feed on very small prey.

WALKING ANEMONES

A sea anemone can 'walk' over rocks. It leans over (1) and grips the rock with its arms (2). Then it somersaults (3) into a new position (4).

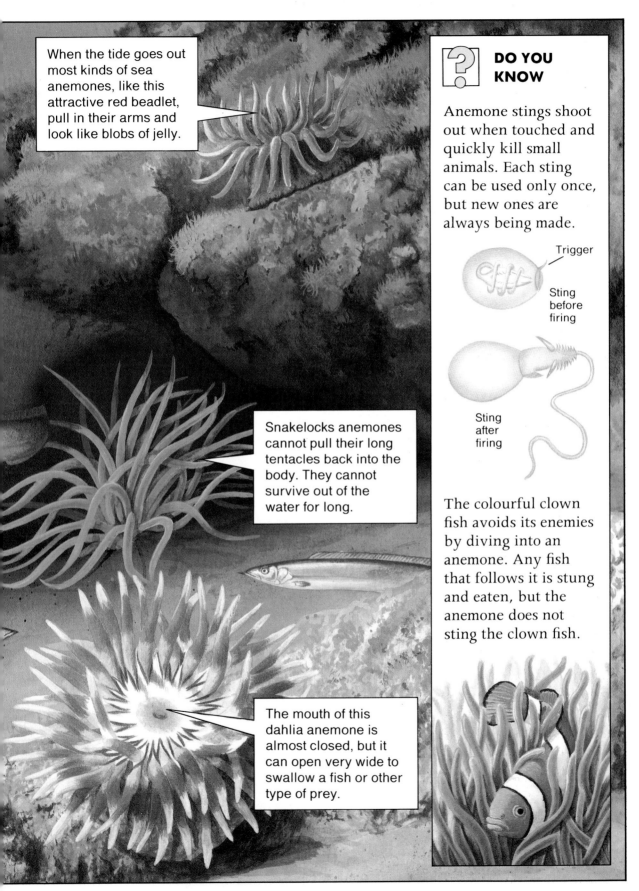

When the tide goes out most kinds of sea anemones, like this attractive red beadlet, pull in their arms and look like blobs of jelly.

DO YOU KNOW

Anemone stings shoot out when touched and quickly kill small animals. Each sting can be used only once, but new ones are always being made.

Trigger

Sting before firing

Sting after firing

Snakelocks anemones cannot pull their long tentacles back into the body. They cannot survive out of the water for long.

The colourful clown fish avoids its enemies by diving into an anemone. Any fish that follows it is stung and eaten, but the anemone does not sting the clown fish.

The mouth of this dahlia anemone is almost closed, but it can open very wide to swallow a fish or other type of prey.

11

Crabs of the seashore

Hundreds of different kinds of crabs live on the seashore. They nearly all have a broad, flat shell and a tiny tail tucked up under the rear end. Most crabs have ten legs. The front legs bear large claws and the other eight are used for scuttling sideways over the sand. Crabs eat other animals, alive or dead, and are very fond of dead fish. They often quarrel over food and sometimes fight fiercely with their claws. A crab often loses a claw in one of these battles, but it can grow a new one quite quickly. Large crabs, such as the edible crab, are good to eat and many are caught for food.

CRAB FACTS

● The biggest crab is the Japanese spider crab. It lives in deep water and its front legs may be 3 metres long.

● The smallest crabs are called pea crabs. Their bodies are only 5 mm across.

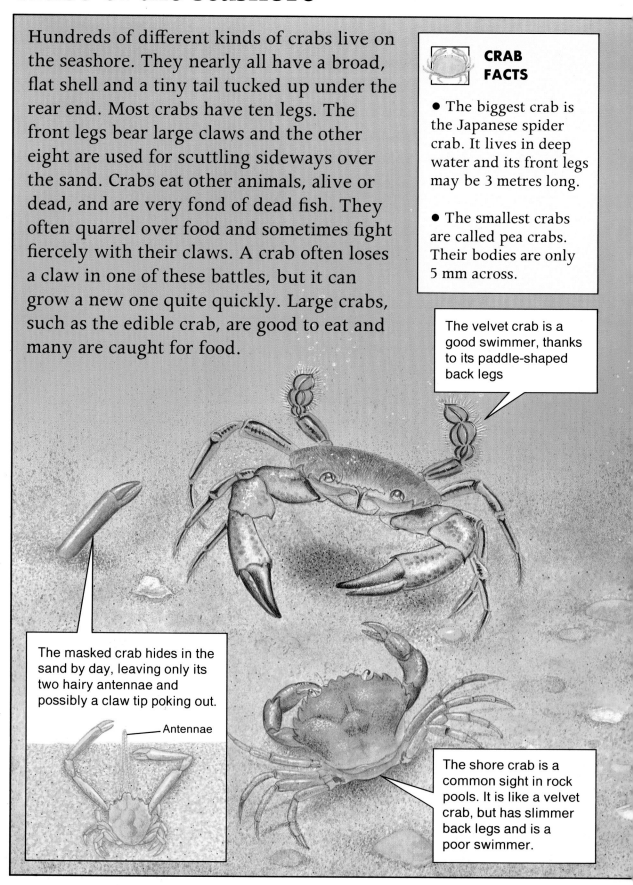

The velvet crab is a good swimmer, thanks to its paddle-shaped back legs

The masked crab hides in the sand by day, leaving only its two hairy antennae and possibly a claw tip poking out.

Antennae

The shore crab is a common sight in rock pools. It is like a velvet crab, but has slimmer back legs and is a poor swimmer.

IN THE MANGROVES

Sharp-clawed mangrove crabs climb all over the tangled bushes of the mangrove swamps, while pale-shelled ghost crabs scuttle over the sand.

Mangrove crab

Ghost crabs

A female crab carries her eggs in a bundle tucked under her tail. The creatures that hatch from the eggs are called larvae and they float to the surface. They do not look like crabs. They change shape several times in the next few months before settling on the seabed and turning into adults.

Crab larvae

Eggs

Edible crabs live on rocky shores. These two are fighting over some mussels and one has lost a claw in the fierce battle.

The hermit crab

The hermit crab is more like a shrimp than a real crab. It has a long, soft body and protects itself by living in the old shell of a whelk or other sea snail. A pair of strong hooks at its rear end hold the crab safely in the shell. As it gets bigger, the hermit crab moves to a bigger shell. Hermit crabs feed mainly on dead animals.

DO YOU KNOW

Sea anemones often grow on a hermit crab's shell, and the crab may even plant them there. The anemones protect the crab with their stings (see page 10). In return, the crab carries them to new feeding grounds.

Sea anemones

A small bristleworm often shares the crab's shell. It steals bits of food but does the crab no other harm.

Before moving house, the hermit crab tests the new shell with its claws to see that it is big enough.

The right claw is bigger than the left one and closes the shell when the crab backs in to rest.

The robber crab

Robber crabs live on tropical beaches. When they are young they live in the sea, but adults cannot swim and they drown if kept underwater for more than a few hours. They feed on dead animals, as well as coconuts and other fruit.

Robber crabs often climb coconut palms, but there is no truth in the story that they throw coconuts to the ground to crack them.

The adult robber crab is about 45 cm long. It has very powerful claws and only four walking legs.

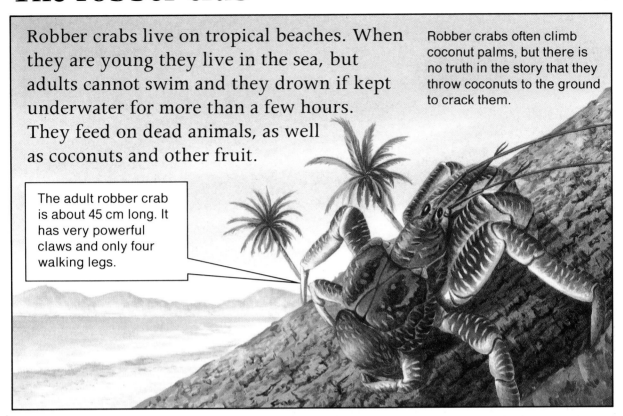

The mud-skipper

Mud-skippers are weird fish that live in coastal swamps in the warmer parts of the world. When the tide goes out they walk and leap over the mud on their arm-like front fins. They can even climb trees. They feed on tiny animals in the mud.

The male mud-skipper waves the big fin on its back like a flag to attract females.

The skimmer

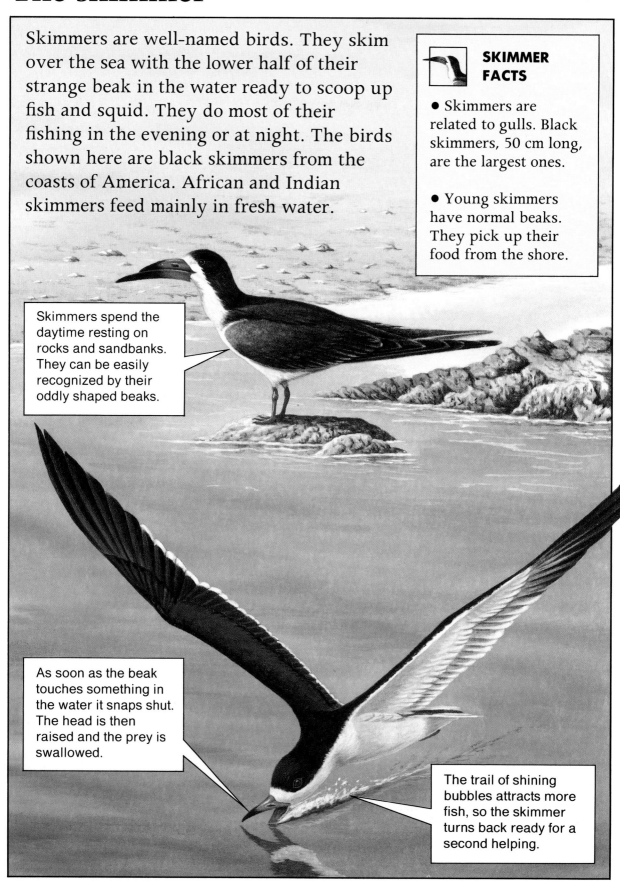

Skimmers are well-named birds. They skim over the sea with the lower half of their strange beak in the water ready to scoop up fish and squid. They do most of their fishing in the evening or at night. The birds shown here are black skimmers from the coasts of America. African and Indian skimmers feed mainly in fresh water.

SKIMMER FACTS

● Skimmers are related to gulls. Black skimmers, 50 cm long, are the largest ones.

● Young skimmers have normal beaks. They pick up their food from the shore.

Skimmers spend the daytime resting on rocks and sandbanks. They can be easily recognized by their oddly shaped beaks.

As soon as the beak touches something in the water it snaps shut. The head is then raised and the prey is swallowed.

The trail of shining bubbles attracts more fish, so the skimmer turns back ready for a second helping.

The white-tailed eagle

The white-tailed eagle is a powerful bird of prey living around the coasts of Eurasia. It also lives by large lakes and rivers. The eagle scoops fish from the surface with its big talons, but rarely plunges right in to the water. Dead sheep also make up a major part of the eagle's diet in some areas, and it may kill small lambs. The birds build untidy nests in tall trees or on high cliffs. They usually lay two eggs, and the chicks fly when they are about 10 weeks old.

? DO YOU KNOW

The white-tailed eagle is a bit of a pirate. It does not always bother to go fishing itself. It often waits for other birds to fly up with fish and then it chases them until they are exhausted and give up their possessions – just like human pirates did in olden days.

Broad wings, nearly 1 metre across, enable the eagle to carry heavy loads back to its nest.

SURVIVAL WATCH

White-tailed eagles were hunted out of existence in the British Isles 80 years ago, but Norwegian birds taken to Scotland in 1975 are now doing well. More are now being released in Ireland.

The eagle's long toes have sharp spines on them to help the bird grip the fish securely as it flies.

Prickly sea urchins

Sea urchins look like pin-cushions with the points sticking outwards. These spines protect the urchins and help them to walk and dig in the sand. Long water-filled suckers also help with movement. There is a thin shell just under the skin. Most sea urchins feed on seaweeds, which they scrape from the rocks using tough jaws on their underside. Others feed on debris which they collect with their suckers. Some urchins have very short spines that look more like fur. The spines all fall off when the animals die.

DO YOU KNOW

Sea urchins start life as tiny swimming larvae like the one shown below. After a while the larvae lose the ability to swim and they sink down to live on the seabed.

CIDARIS

Cidaris walks over the seabed on its stout spines. These are up to 14 cm long. They are purple at first but turn grey as they age.

The shells of edible sea urchins, up to 15 cm across, make good ornaments. A spine was attached to each pimple in life.

Gulls and other sea-birds often attack rock urchins to get at the soft flesh. The broken shells are often seen on the shore.

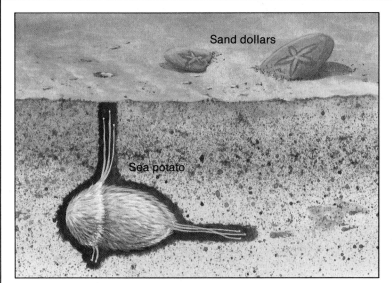

Sand dollars

Sea potato

UNUSUAL URCHINS

Sand dollars are flat, biscuit-shaped urchins with short, fur-like spines. They eat scraps of food as they plough through the sand. Sea potatoes burrow in the sand. Some of their long suckers collect food, and others reach the surface to allow the urchin to breathe.

Rock urchins live in rock pools. They hide themselves with bits of broken shells and seaweed, held on by their suckers.

URCHIN FACTS

● There are about 600 kinds of sea urchins, ranging from 1 cm to 45 cm in diameter, including their spines.

● The spines of some sea urchins can cause painful wounds if you tread on them.

Edible sea urchins normally live below low tide level or in rock pools. The soft inner parts are good to eat.

Mussels galore

Deep blue mussel shells cover the rocks on many seashores. The mussels are anchored by tough threads and they never need to move. They feed by straining tiny scraps of food from the water brought in by the tide.

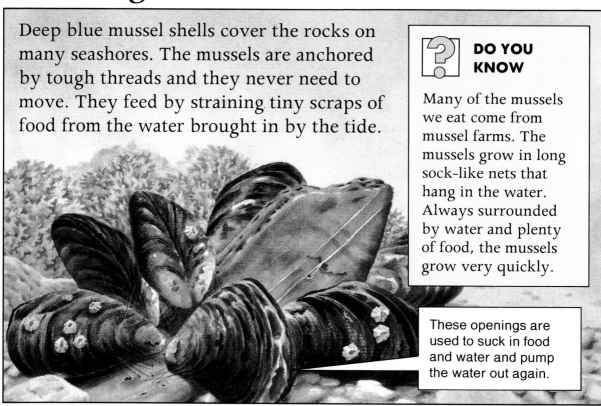

? DO YOU KNOW

Many of the mussels we eat come from mussel farms. The mussels grow in long sock-like nets that hang in the water. Always surrounded by water and plenty of food, the mussels grow very quickly.

These openings are used to suck in food and water and pump the water out again.

The pearly oyster

Oysters are shellfish whose shells are firmly cemented to underwater rocks. They feed by straining food particles from the water. People harvest tonnes of them each year for food. Oysters are also famous for their pearls, which are used in jewellery.

The upper half of the oyster's crinkly shell is flat and sits on the saucer-shaped lower half like a lid.

? DO YOU KNOW

A pearl is produced when a sand grain gets inside the shell and irritates the oyster's skin. The oyster covers the sand with layers of smooth, shiny material and this becomes the pearl.

Pearl

The leisurely limpet

Limpets are sea snails that live on rocky shores. When the tide comes in they glide over the rocks to graze on the seaweeds. When the tide goes out each limpet returns to its own spot and settles down to rest.

Circular marks show where limpets once lived and their hard shells wore grooves in the rocks.

When out of the water at low tide, the limpet uses its strong muscles to pull the shell tight against the rock. It is extremely hard to pull the animal off.

The slipper limpet

The slipper limpet gets its name because its shell looks rather like a slipper. It is a sea snail, but it does not move about. It fixes itself to stones or other shells at about low tide level and feeds by filtering tiny food particles from the water.

DO YOU KNOW

Young slipper limpets are all males, but they turn into females as they get older.

Slipper limpets ruin oyster beds by settling on the oysters and stopping them feeding.

Slipper limpets form chains or clusters as big as a man's fist. The smallest and youngest ones in the group are all males.

The comical puffin

The puffin is famous for its big, colourful beak and its comical, clown-like walk. It looks rather like a penguin when walking but, unlike penguins, it can also fly. Puffins eat fish and often go far out to sea in the winter. In the summer they breed on the coasts of the North Atlantic and on islands in the Arctic Ocean.

Puffin numbers fell fast in many areas in the 1960s. They have now risen again, especially in the colder regions. These changes may be linked to changes in climate which affect the fish that the puffins eat.

Puffins nest in holes on the tops of cliffs. They often use old rabbit burrows. Females lay just one egg as a rule.

Puffins feed mainly on sand-eels. They can carry up to 30 of these slender fish in their big beaks at one time.

The puffin uses its broad webbed feet to change direction and slow itself down when it is flying.

A puffin is about 20 cm high. It flies well, although its plump body looks too heavy for its narrow wings.

Feathery fanworms

Vast numbers of worms live on the seashore. They hide under the sand when the tide goes out, but wading birds still find them and eat them. The worms come out to feed when the tide comes in. Many are called fanworms. Instead of hunting, these worms sit still and strain food from the water with fans of feathery tentacles. Most fanworms live in tubes, which often stick out of the sand when the tide is out.

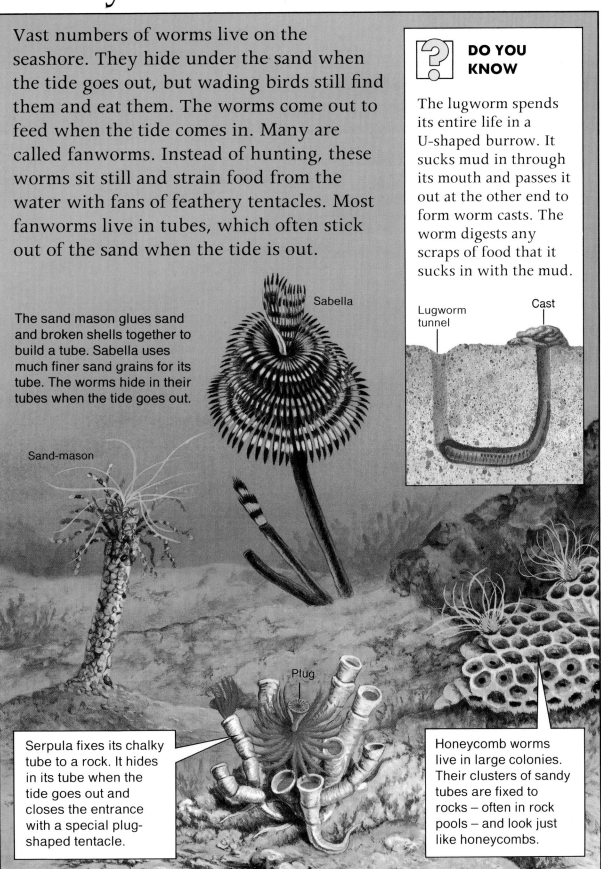

DO YOU KNOW

The lugworm spends its entire life in a U-shaped burrow. It sucks mud in through its mouth and passes it out at the other end to form worm casts. The worm digests any scraps of food that it sucks in with the mud.

Lugworm tunnel

Cast

Sabella

The sand mason glues sand and broken shells together to build a tube. Sabella uses much finer sand grains for its tube. The worms hide in their tubes when the tide goes out.

Sand-mason

Plug

Serpula fixes its chalky tube to a rock. It hides in its tube when the tide goes out and closes the entrance with a special plug-shaped tentacle.

Honeycomb worms live in large colonies. Their clusters of sandy tubes are fixed to rocks – often in rock pools – and look just like honeycombs.

Long-legged wading birds

Huge flocks of long-legged wading birds visit the seashores, especially in the winter. They come to feed on the millions of worms, shellfish and shrimp-like creatures that live in the sand, mud and shallow water along the shore. Many of these birds have very long beaks, with which they feel for prey in the sand or mud. Others catch their food by sweeping their beaks through the water.

Many waders are great travellers. They spend the summer in the far north and then fly south to spend the winter by the sea.

The black-winged stilt's extremely long, thin legs enable it to wade in deeper water than other waders to find its food.

The avocet searches for crustaceans in the shallows by sweeping its slightly up-turned beak from side to side through the water.

The spoonbill has a spoon-shaped beak, which it sweeps through the water to catch shrimps and other small animals.

? **DO YOU KNOW**

The long beaks of some waders enable them to find food deep in the mud. Short-beaked waders find food near the surface.

Despite their name, oystercatchers do not catch oysters. Cockles and mussels are their favourite foods.

The redshank scampers over the shore and sweeps its thin beak from side to side through the sand or mud to find food.

The ringed plover usually nests on the shore, where its spotted eggs are well camouflaged amongst the sand and shingle.

The turnstone gets its name because it uses its beak to turn over stones and other objects while it is searching for food.

Claw-waving fiddler crabs

The male fiddler crab has one claw very much bigger than the other. The big claw is often brightly coloured and it is called a fiddle. The crab uses it like a flag, waving it up and down to tell other males to keep away. The claw is also waved vigorously to attract females. Fiddler crabs live in burrows on tropical seashores, especially in muddy areas near river mouths. They leave their burrows only when the tide goes out.

DO YOU KNOW

Each of the many kinds of fiddler crab has its own signalling system. Females are attracted only to males of their own kind.

Some fiddlers make sounds by rubbing the large claw against a row of teeth on the front of the shell.

The female is less colourful than the male. She has two normal claws and uses them both to get food from the mud.

The colour of the crab's shell is always changing. It is particularly bright when the male is waving to a female.

Fiddler crabs stay near their burrows. When the tide comes in each crab goes into its burrow and closes the entrance with a lump of mud.

The crabs feed by picking up sand or mud in their small claws and licking tiny animals and other food from it.

The crusty barnacle

Barnacles form crusty white coverings on many seaside rocks. They look quite dead when the tide is out, but they open up to feed when it returns. Young barnacles swim in the sea for a time before settling down.

The tent-like shell opens underwater and feathery legs comb tiny scraps of food from the water.

? DO YOU KNOW

Barnacles are related to crabs, although an adult barnacle does not look like a crab at all. A young barnacle (below) looks quite like a baby crab until it settles down and forms its shell.

The tunnelling piddock

The piddock is a seashell that digs its own tomb. It uses the spiny front end of its shell to tunnel slowly into underwater rocks. It can live for a long time, but it can never turn round and tunnel out again.

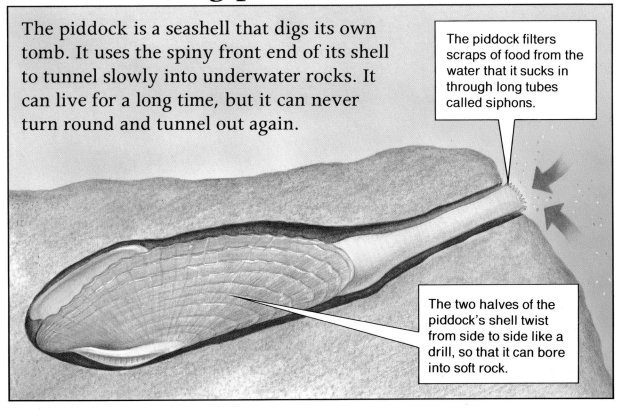

The piddock filters scraps of food from the water that it sucks in through long tubes called siphons.

The two halves of the piddock's shell twist from side to side like a drill, so that it can bore into soft rock.

The poisonous weever

Weever fish burrow in sand with just their poison spines exposed. They live in shallow water near the coasts of Europe and Africa and eat shrimps and other small animals.

The spines on the weever's back cause a lot of pain if they are trodden on.

The clinging goby

Gobies are small fish that live in coastal areas all over the world. Several kinds are common in rock pools. They have two fins on the top of the body, the front one being rather spiny.

DO YOU KNOW

The world's smallest fish is a type of goby. It is only 15 mm long.

Some gobies use empty seashells as nests for their eggs. Male gobies always guard the eggs.

The goby's lower fins are joined together to form a sucker with which the fish is able to cling to rocks. This stops it from being swept away by the current.

The guillemot

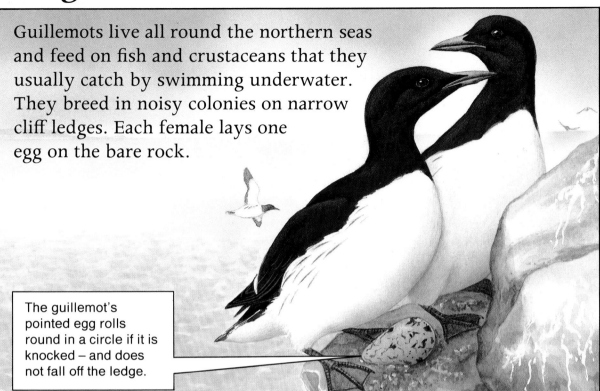

Guillemots live all round the northern seas and feed on fish and crustaceans that they usually catch by swimming underwater. They breed in noisy colonies on narrow cliff ledges. Each female lays one egg on the bare rock.

The guillemot's pointed egg rolls round in a circle if it is knocked – and does not fall off the ledge.

The cormorant

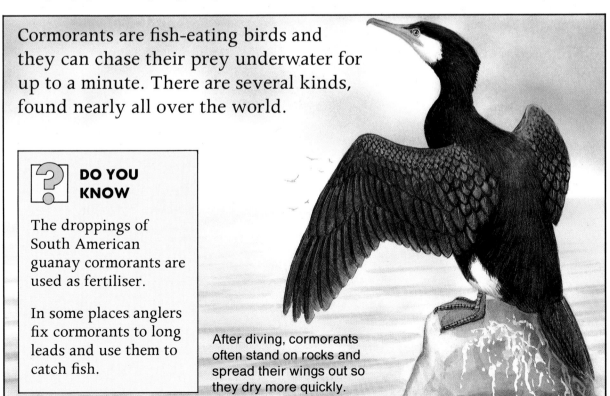

Cormorants are fish-eating birds and they can chase their prey underwater for up to a minute. There are several kinds, found nearly all over the world.

? **DO YOU KNOW**

The droppings of South American guanay cormorants are used as fertiliser.

In some places anglers fix cormorants to long leads and use them to catch fish.

After diving, cormorants often stand on rocks and spread their wings out so they dry more quickly.

The scarlet ibis

The scarlet ibis is one of the world's most colourful birds. It lives in big flocks in the muddy mangrove swamps along the coasts and rivers of tropical America. It uses its long, curved beak to catch fish and to dig for crabs and other small animals in the mud. Ibises build large, untidy nests out of sticks in the waterside trees.

Scarlet ibises look like showers of red confetti when they arrive to roost in the mangroves in the evening. They flap their wings in unison, as if they were all tied together.

The young scarlet ibis has black and white feathers. It does not get its brilliant red coat until it is over a year old.

The fairy penguin

The fairy penguin is the world's smallest penguin. It lives on rocky coasts in New Zealand and Australia. It feeds on fish in the coastal waters by day, and comes ashore to sleep at night. Unlike most other penguins, it does not form crowded colonies, and each pair likes to nest alone.

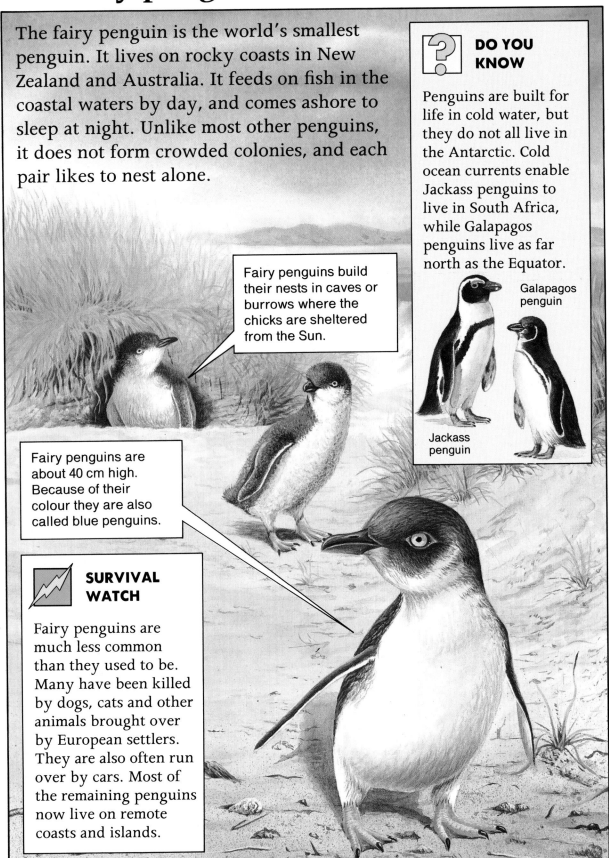

DO YOU KNOW

Penguins are built for life in cold water, but they do not all live in the Antarctic. Cold ocean currents enable Jackass penguins to live in South Africa, while Galapagos penguins live as far north as the Equator.

Galapagos penguin

Jackass penguin

Fairy penguins build their nests in caves or burrows where the chicks are sheltered from the Sun.

Fairy penguins are about 40 cm high. Because of their colour they are also called blue penguins.

SURVIVAL WATCH

Fairy penguins are much less common than they used to be. Many have been killed by dogs, cats and other animals brought over by European settlers. They are also often run over by cars. Most of the remaining penguins now live on remote coasts and islands.

Colourful seashells

Seashells are the cases of soft-bodied animals called molluscs or shellfish. When the animals die, the empty shells are washed up on the beach. There are thousands of different kinds, belonging to two main groups – sea snails and bivalves. Sea snails have coiled shells like land snails. Bivalve shells have two halves hinged together. Sea snails have mouths full of small, sharp teeth, with which they eat seaweeds or other animals. Bivalves strain small scraps of food from the water.

DO YOU KNOW

Colourful seashells, like the tiger cowrie shown below, have long been used as ornaments and for making jewellery. In some places shells were once used as money. The china-like cowrie shells were the favourites because they are smooth and easy to handle.

Tiger cowrie

Buried in the sand, the tellin uses two long siphons to suck in rubbish from the seabed and pump out what it doesn't eat.

The cockle only has short siphons, and it buries itself just below the surface. It sucks in water and strains food from it.

Cockles and most other bivalves burrow in mud and sand with the aid of a muscle called the foot.

SEASHELL FACTS

● The sand on some seashores consists almost entirely of tiny pieces of seashells.

● The world's biggest seashell belongs to the giant clam of the Indian and Pacific Oceans. The shell can be over 1 metre wide and a living giant clam can weigh 250 kg.

Giant clam

Murex sea snails contain a strong purple dye. The Romans used it to colour their ceremonial robes.

The queen conch is one of the biggest of the many sea snails. Its 30-cm shell has been used as a kind of trumpet.

Scallops can swim by flapping their hinged shells. They have simple eyes around the edge of the body.

Some tropical cones are very dangerous. Their teeth carry a deadly poison that can kill a person.

Slithering sea slugs

Sea slugs, like their land-living cousins, are really snails without shells. Some sea slugs live close to the shore, but others live in very deep water. Some spend all their lives swimming in the open ocean. Sea slugs include some of the most colourful of all sea creatures. Most sea slugs feed on other small animals, including sea anemones and sponges, but there are some vegetarian kinds that only feed on seaweeds.

? DO YOU KNOW

A few kinds of sea slugs eat small sea anemones without making them fire their stings (see page 11). The sea slugs store the stings in their bodies and fire them at their own enemies. Instead of a tasty meal, a predator ends up with a mouthful of stings.

The sea lemon is one of the commonest sea slugs. It feeds on small sponges and can often be found in rock pools. It is 7 cm long.

The grey sea slug is up to 8 cm long and eats sea anemones. It lays its eggs in long white ribbons.

The sea lemon breathes by means of these tufts of leaf-like gills. It can pull them into its body.

These worm-like flaps take oxygen from the water for breathing. They may also carry unfired stings from the slug's prey (see above).

The spiny lobster

Spiny lobsters, or crawfish, live in rocky places – usually below low tide level. Up to 45 cm long, they are a popular food. They eat other animals.

The spiny lobster has no big claws. It defends itself by lashing out with its long, spiny antennae.

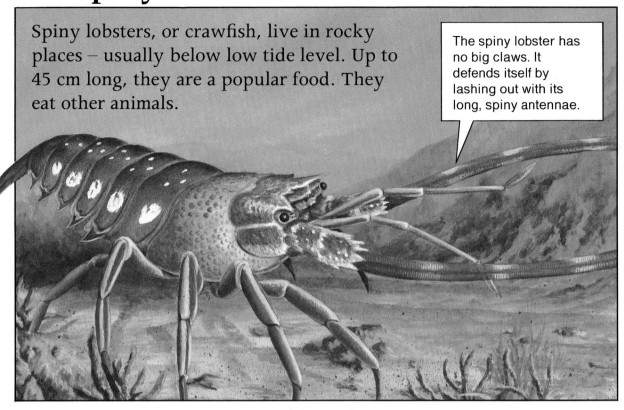

The curious king crab

King crabs, or horseshoe crabs, live on sandy beaches in the warmer parts of the world. They can swim on their backs, but spend most of their time digging in the sand in search of worms and other small animals.

KING CRAB FACTS

● Adult king crabs are about 60 cm long.

● The king crab is not really a crab at all. It is more closely related to land-dwelling spiders and scorpions.

The spiky tail pushes the animal along, and also turns it the right way up if it is over-turned by waves.

Shrimps, prawns and scampi

Shrimps and prawns are related to crabs, but they are much slimmer and usually swim well. They have five pairs of legs, with pincers on the front ones and sometimes on others as well. The back half of the body carries small, feathery limbs that are used as paddles when swimming. The tail fan can be opened out and used as a flipper.

These animals eat whatever they can find on the seabed. We eat a lot of them ourselves. Live ones are mostly brown, but they turn pink when cooked.

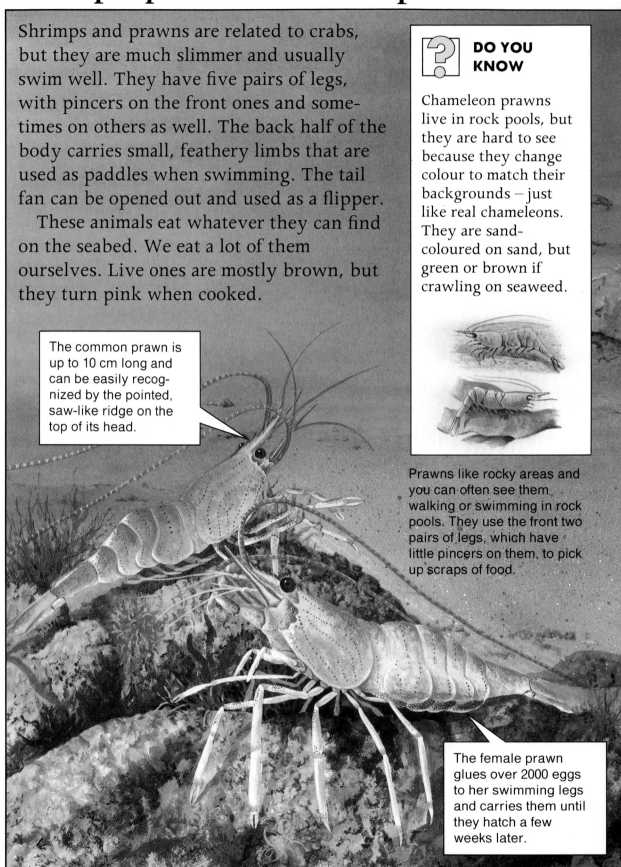

DO YOU KNOW

Chameleon prawns live in rock pools, but they are hard to see because they change colour to match their backgrounds – just like real chameleons. They are sand-coloured on sand, but green or brown if crawling on seaweed.

The common prawn is up to 10 cm long and can be easily recognized by the pointed, saw-like ridge on the top of its head.

Prawns like rocky areas and you can often see them walking or swimming in rock pools. They use the front two pairs of legs, which have little pincers on them, to pick up scraps of food.

The female prawn glues over 2000 eggs to her swimming legs and carries them until they hatch a few weeks later.

The Norway lobster likes muddy areas and does not often come to the shore. It uses its big pincers for defence and collects food with the smaller ones. The Norway lobster's flesh is called scampi.

The Norway lobster is up to 15 cm long and does not swim. Its rather flat body is designed for crawling over sand and mud.

The skeleton shrimp, or ghost shrimp, is not a real shrimp at all. It clings to seaweed and grabs small animals with its claws.

The common shrimp looks like a prawn, but it has no toothed ridge on its head and its front legs are much stouter. The shrimp hides in the sand by day and hunts for animal food at night.

Seashores in danger

Many seashores are littered with plastic bottles and ropes and other rubbish, but the most serious problem is oil. Huge ships carry oil across the oceans, and if there is an accident thousands of tonnes of oil may leak into the sea. Tides wash the oil on to the shore and, as well as spoiling the beaches for holidays, it destroys the seashore plants and animals. We can clean a sandy beach quite quickly, but nature needs many years to clean the rocks and replace the lost seaweeds and animal life.

 SAVING SEABIRDS

The worst casualties of oil spills are puffins and other seabirds that have to dive through the oil to catch their fish. Covered with the slimy oil, they die if they get no help. Luckily, we can clean them with special detergents or soap. As long as the birds have not swallowed too much oil they will survive. They are kept in captivity until their feathers have regained their natural water-proofing – and then they are released.

Oil leaking from a damaged tanker forms a thick black sheet on the surface of the water. Detergents help to break this up, while people and machines struggle to remove the sticky oil from the beach.

Useful words

Antenna   One of the feelers of crabs and their relatives that help the animals to pick up smells and to find their way around.

Bivalve   The name given to any of the seashells, such as cockles and mussels, that are in two parts with a hinge along one edge.

Camouflage   The way in which animals avoid the attention of their enemies by resembling their surroundings or blending in with them. The animals are then not easy to recognize.

Coast   The edge of the land, where it meets the sea.

Crustacean   Any member of the crab and lobster group of animals – hard-shelled creatures with lots of legs.

Eurasia   The name given to the large land mass that consists of the continents of Europe and Asia.

Fin   Any of the limbs or other flaps that fish use for swimming.

Gill   The breathing organ of fish, crustaceans, and many other water-dwelling animals. It takes life-giving oxygen from the water flowing over it.

Larva   The name given to a young animal, particularly a crustacean or an insect, that is noticeably different in shape from the adult.

Marine   Concerning the sea.

Mollusc   Any animal of the group containing slugs, snails, and bivalves.

Molluscs have soft bodies and no legs, and most are enclosed in a hard shell.

Scavenger   An animal that feeds mainly on dead matter – especially one that clears up the remains of another animal's meal.

Shellfish   The name given to various hard-shelled sea creatures, especially cockles and mussels and their relatives. Crabs and other crustaceans are also commonly known as shellfish.

Shingle   Coarse gravel and pebbles, up to about 6 cm across, usually found on the upper parts of the seashore.

Siphon   A tube through which many molluscs suck water into their bodies for breathing and feeding. Many have a second siphon for pumping the water out again.

Strand line   The line of debris left on the shore at high-tide level.

Tentacle   A soft, finger-like projection that is found near the mouth of many animals, including sea anemones. Tentacles are normally used for catching food.

Tide   The regular rise and fall of sea level, which floods and then uncovers the seashore twice every day.

Tropical   To do with the tropics – the warm areas of the world on each side of the Equator.

Wader   The name given to various long-legged birds that feed on marshland and in shallow water at the edge of the sea

Index